HAVE YOU
SEEN THIS
WIZARD?

EASY PIANO

MUSIC BY JOHN WILLIAMS
PATRICK DOYLE
NICHOLAS HOOPER
& ALEXANDRE DESPLAT

SHEET MUSIC
FROM THE
COMPLETE
FILM SERIES

Arranged by Dan Coates

Alfred

Produced by
Alfred Music Publishing Co., Inc.
P.O. Box 10003
Van Nuys, CA 91410-0003
alfred.com

Printed in USA.

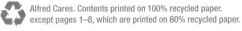

Alfred Cares. Contents printed on 100% recycled paper. except pages 1–8, which are printed on 60% recycled paper.

ISBN-10: 0-7390-8772-X
ISBN-13: 978-0-7390-8772-5

Hedwig's Theme
from *Harry Potter and the Sorcerer's Stone*

Music by **JOHN WILLIAMS**

Arr. by Dan Coates

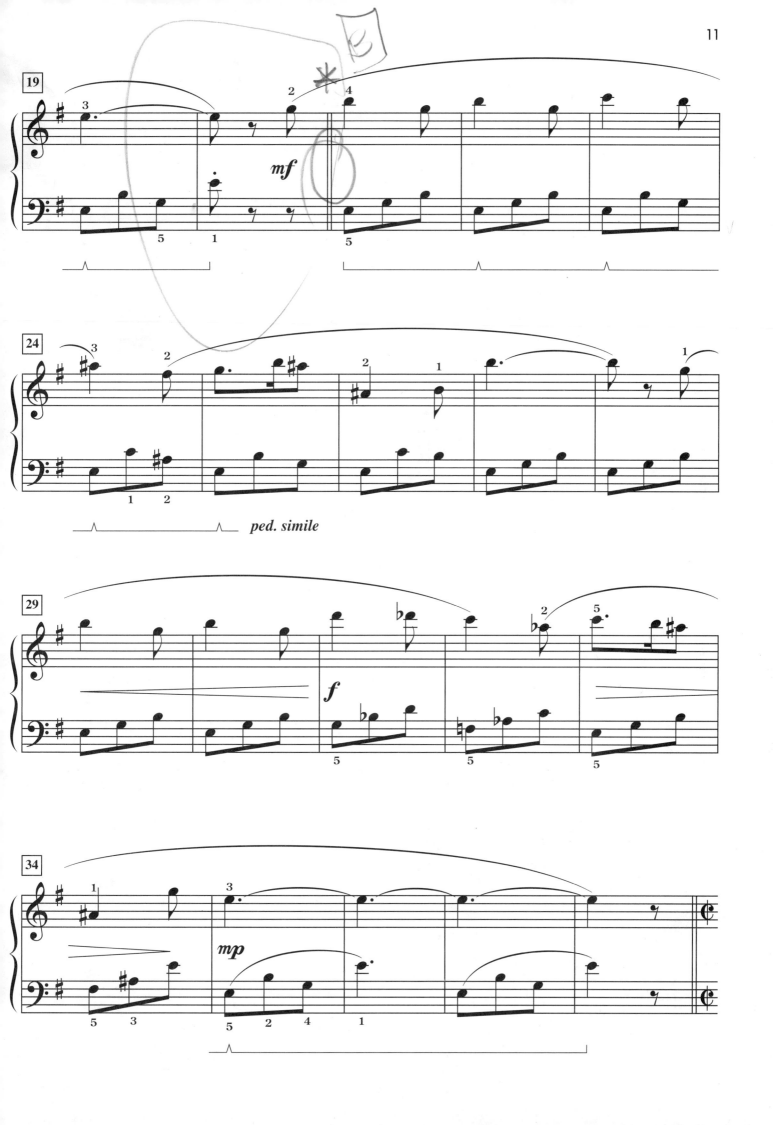

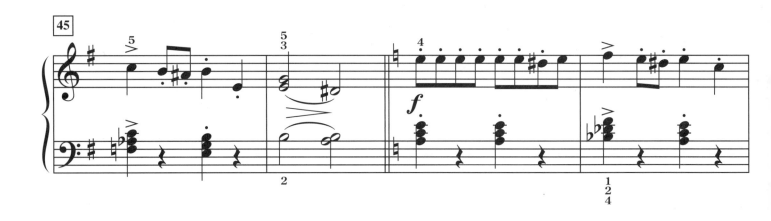

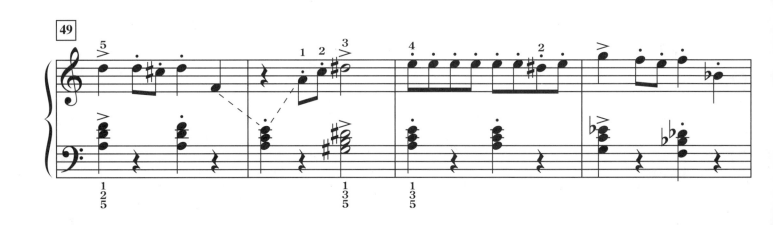

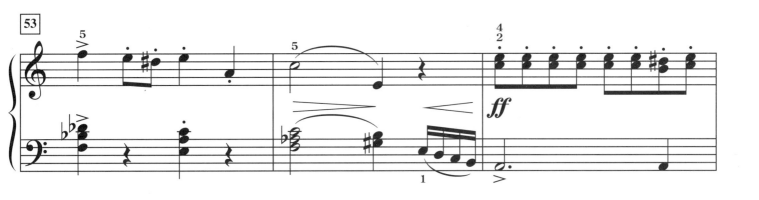

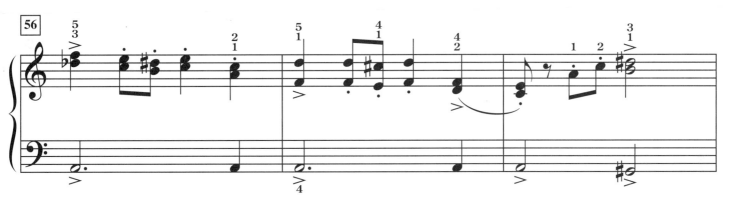

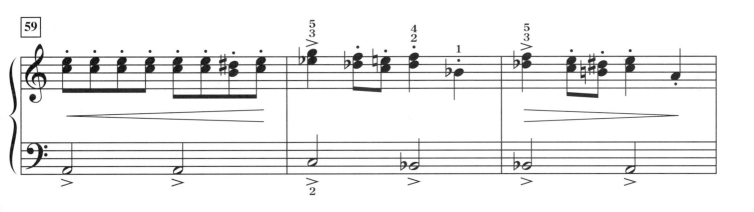

Harry's Wondrous World

from *Harry Potter and the Sorcerer's Stone*

Music by **JOHN WILLIAMS**

Arr. by Dan Coates

Family Portrait

from *Harry Potter and the Sorcerer's Stone*

Music by **JOHN WILLIAMS**
Arr. by Dan Coates

Nimbus 2000

from *Harry Potter and the Sorcerer's Stone*

Music by **JOHN WILLIAMS**

Arr. by Dan Coates

Voldemort
from *Harry Potter and the Sorcerer's Stone*

Music by **JOHN WILLIAMS**

Arr. by Dan Coates

Sinister

Diagon Alley
from *Harry Potter and the Sorcerer's Stone*

Music by **JOHN WILLIAMS**

Arr. by Dan Coates

Joyously

Leaving Hogwarts

from *Harry Potter and the Sorcerer's Stone*

Music by **JOHN WILLIAMS**

Arr. by Dan Coates

The Chamber of Secrets

from *Harry Potter and the Chamber of Secrets*

Music by **JOHN WILLIAMS**
Arr. by Dan Coates

Mysteriously

Fawkes the Phoenix
from *Harry Potter and the Chamber of Secrets*

Music by **JOHN WILLIAMS**
Arr. by Dan Coates

Hagrid the Professor

from *Harry Potter and the Prisoner of Azkaban*

Music by **JOHN WILLIAMS**

Arr. by Dan Coates

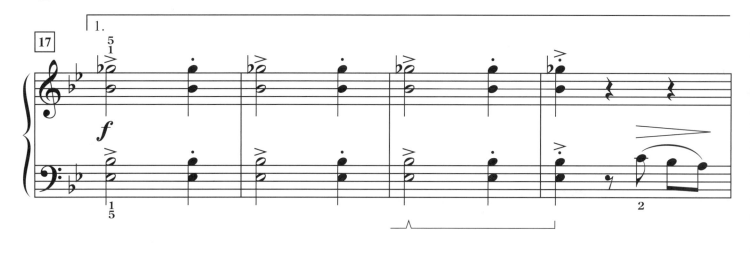

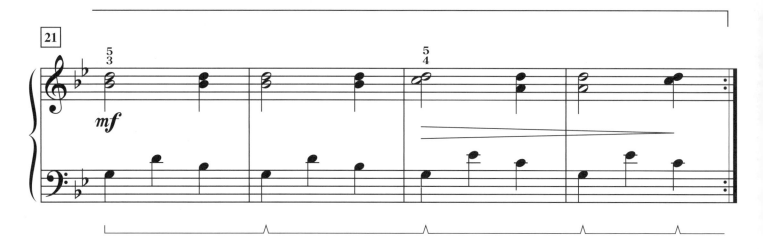

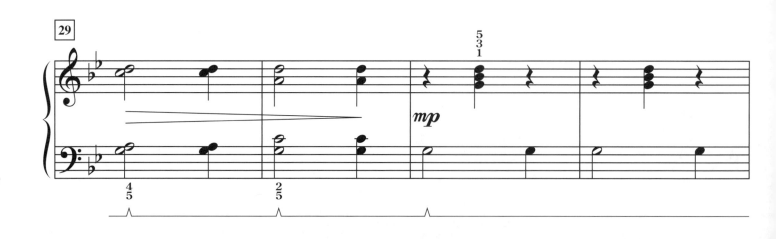

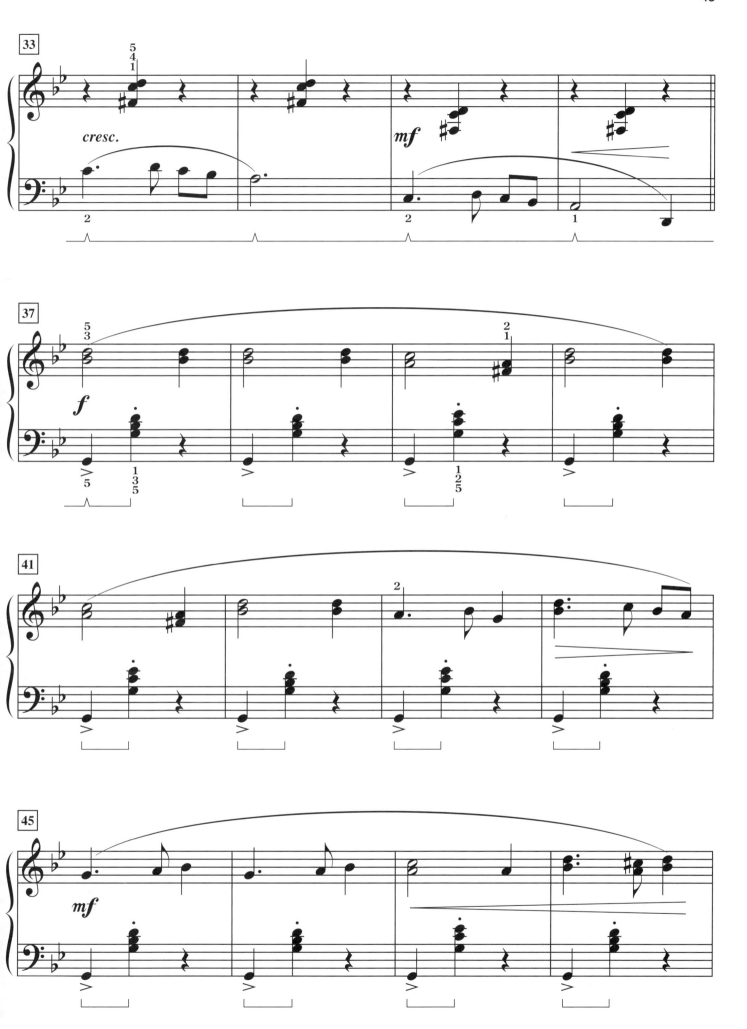

Double Trouble

from *Harry Potter and the Prisoner of Azkaban*

By **JOHN WILLIAMS**

Arr. by Dan Coates

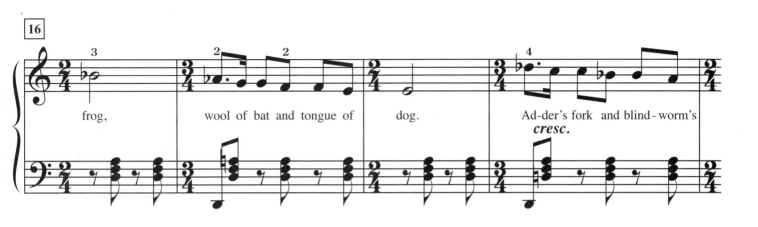

Dou - ble, dou - ble toil and trou - ble; some - thing wick - ed this way comes!

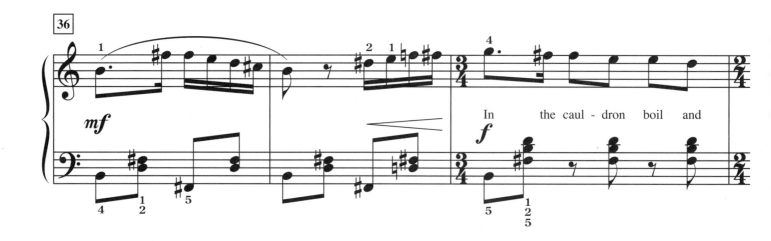

In the caul - dron boil and

bake, fil - let of a fen - ny snake.

Scale of drag - on, tooth of wolf, witch - es' mum - my, maw and

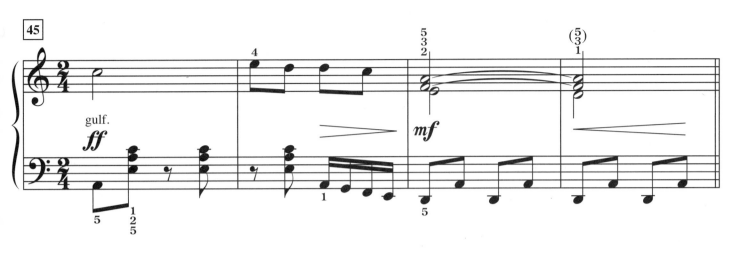

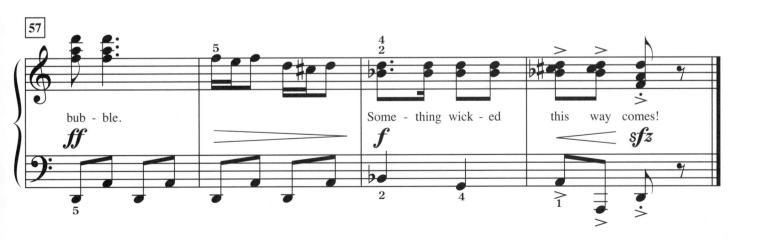

Buckbeak's Flight

from *Harry Potter and the Prisoner of Azkaban*

By **JOHN WILLIAMS**
Arr. by Dan Coates

Moderately slow

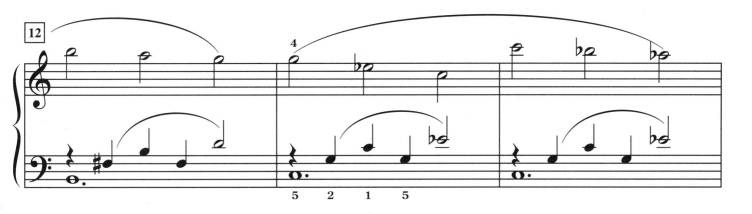

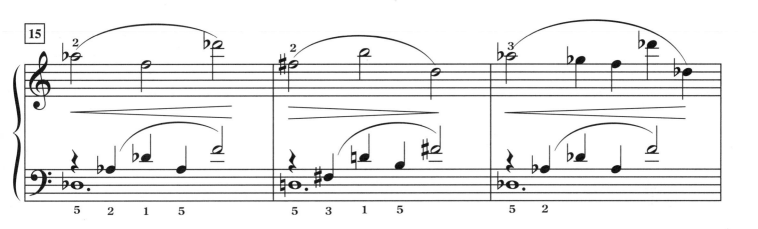

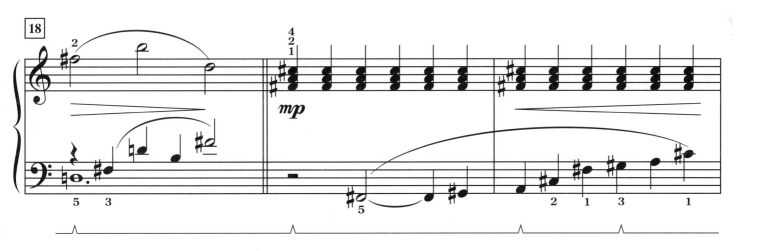

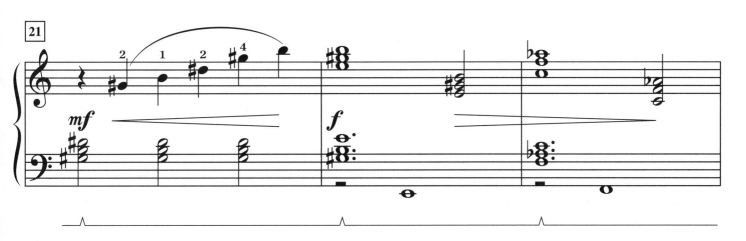

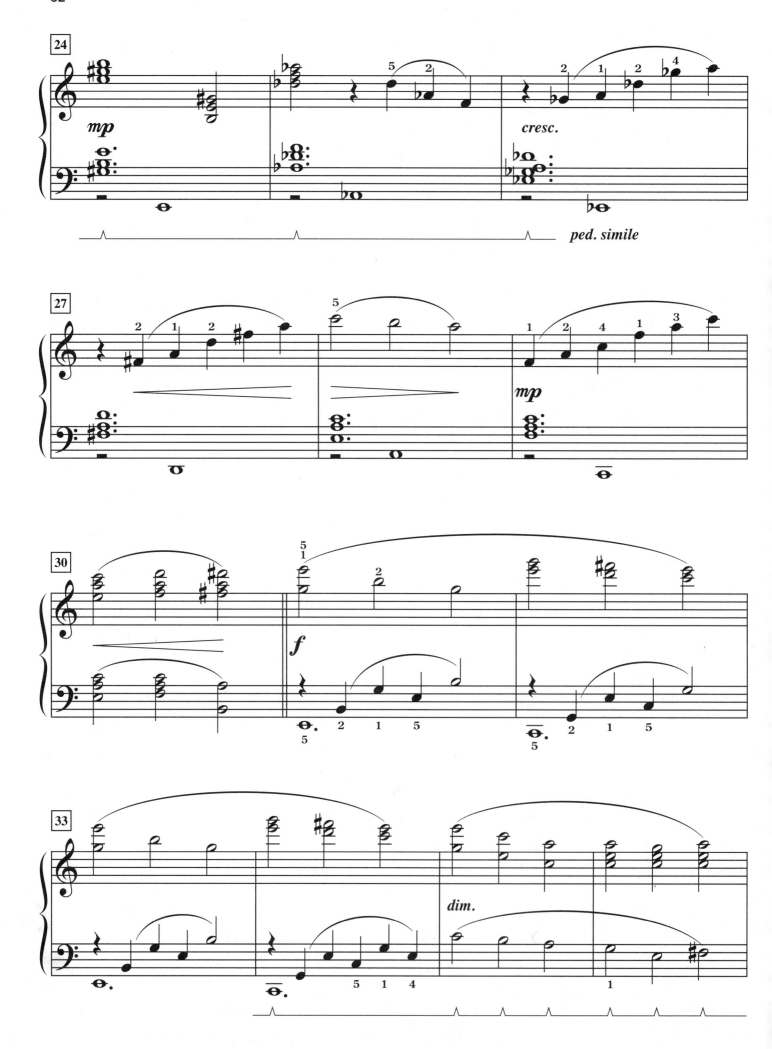

Harry in Winter

from *Harry Potter and the Goblet of Fire*

Music by Patrick Doyle

Arr. by Dan Coates

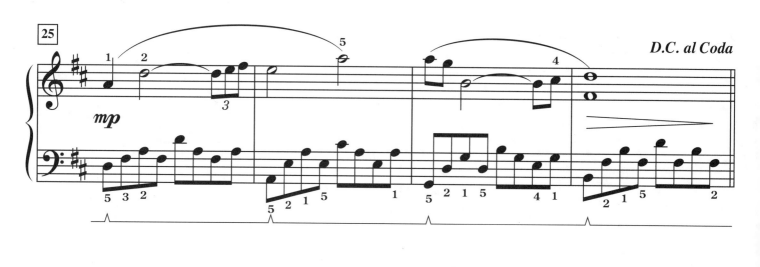

D.C. al Coda

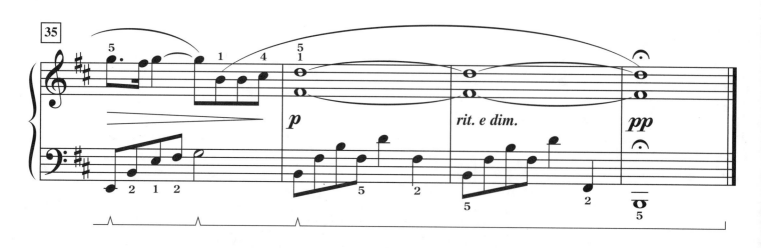

Potter Waltz
from *Harry Potter and the Goblet of Fire*

Music by Patrick Doyle

Arr. by Dan Coates

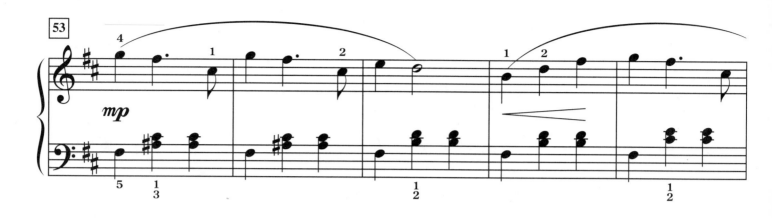

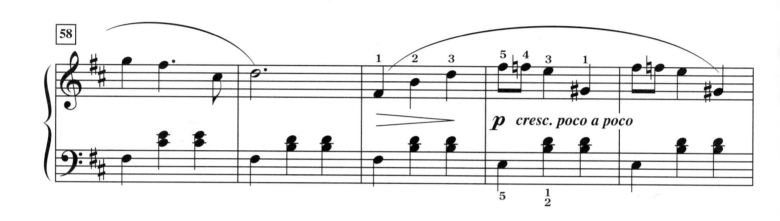

D.S. al Coda

Hogwarts March

from *Harry Potter and the Goblet of Fire*

Music by Patrick Doyle

Arr. by Dan Coates

This Is the Night

from *Harry Potter and the Goblet of Fire*

Words and Music by Jarvis Cocker
Arr. by Dan Coates

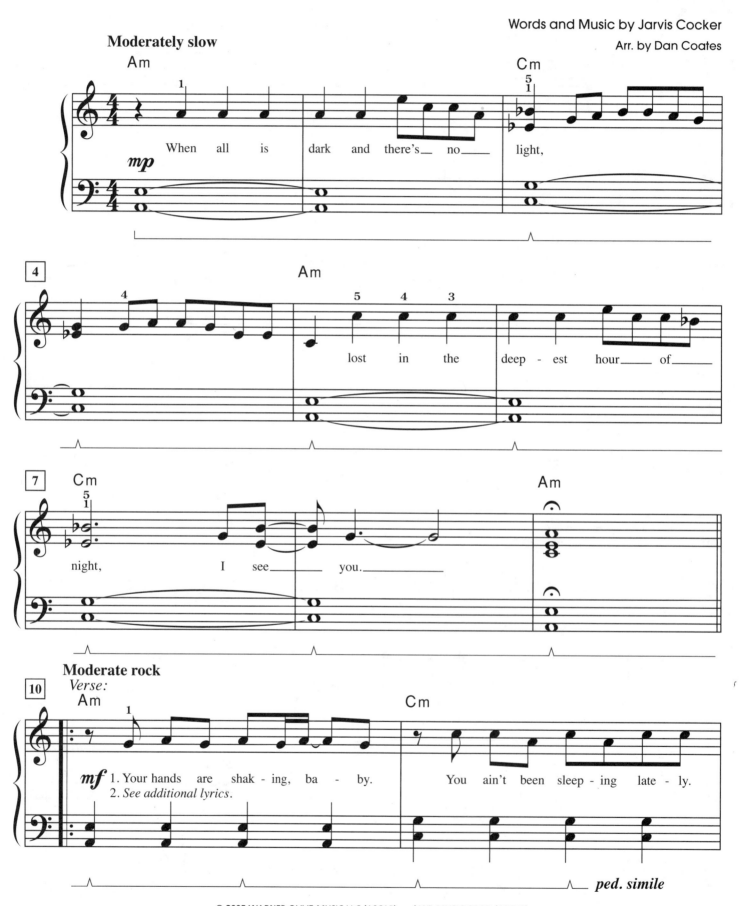

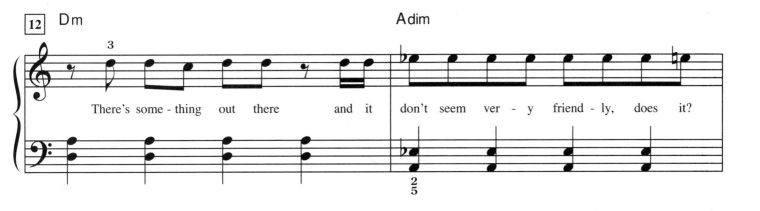

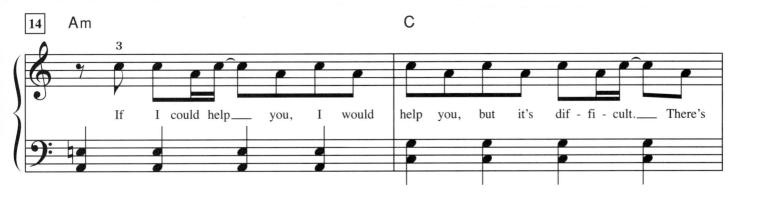

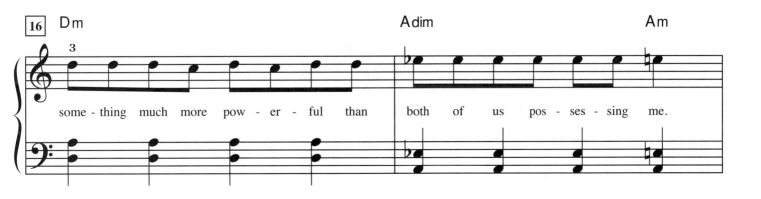

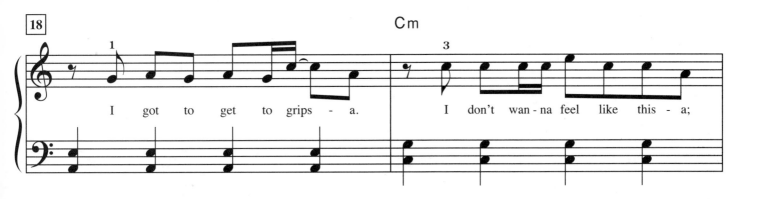

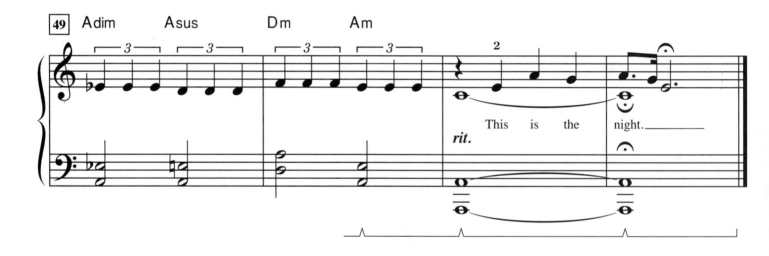

Verse 2:
There was a time I would have walked on burning coals for you,
Sailed across the ocean blue,
Climbed the highest mountain just to call your name.
The moon throws down its light and cuts me to the quick tonight.
A change is in the air and nothing will ever be the same.
You still look good to me,
Ooh, but you're no good for me.
I close my eyes and squeeze you from my consciousness.
And in the morning when I wake,
I walk the line, I walk it straight,
But the morning's so many miles away.
Good God now!
(To Chorus:)

Fireworks
from *Harry Potter and the Order of the Phoenix*

Music by Nicholas Hooper

Arr. by Dan Coates

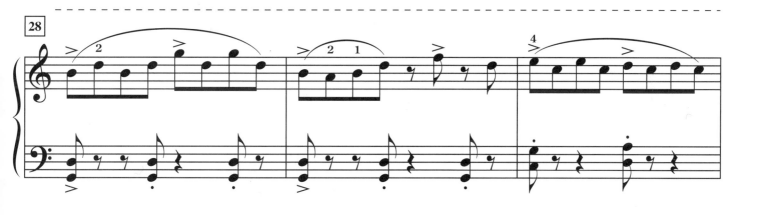

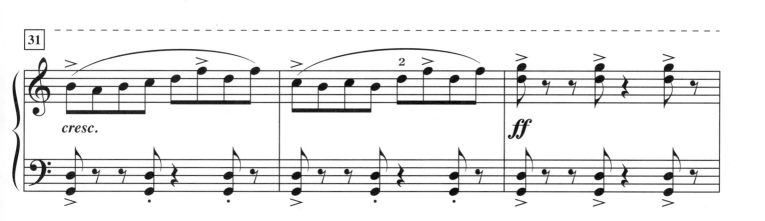

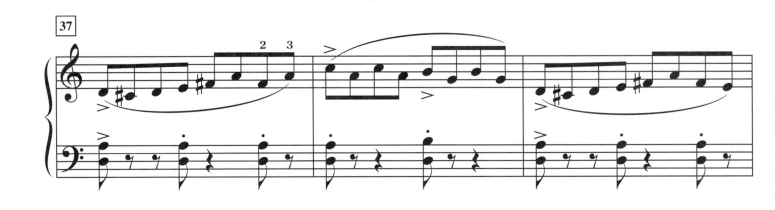

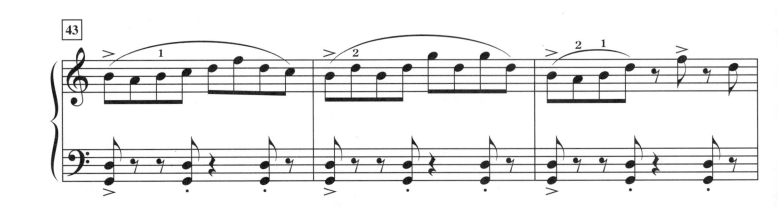

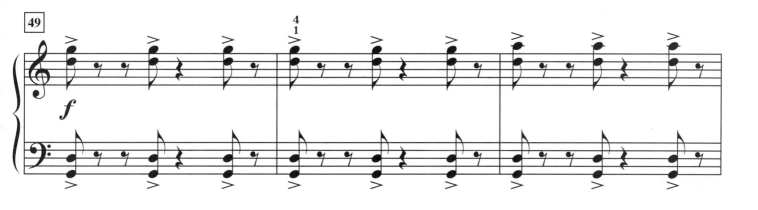

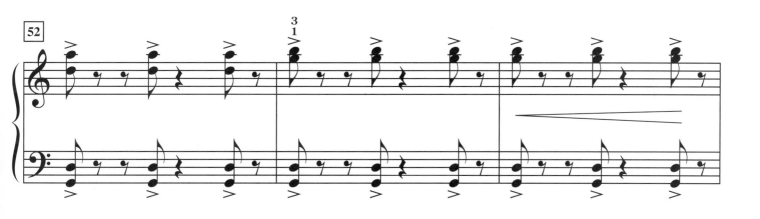

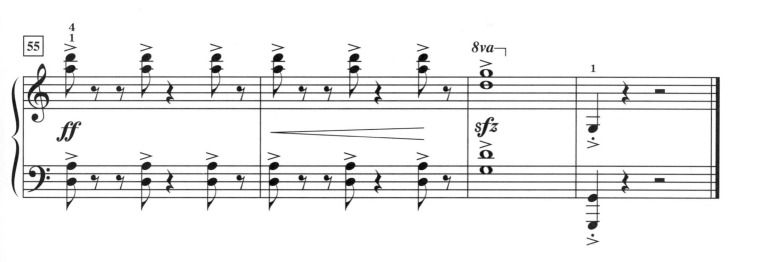

Professor Umbridge
from *Harry Potter and the Order of the Phoenix*

Music by Nicholas Hooper

Arr. by Dan Coates

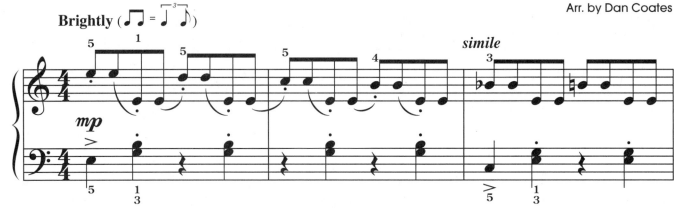

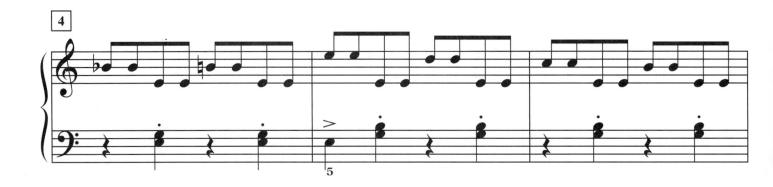

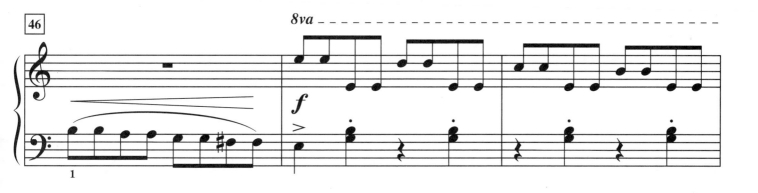

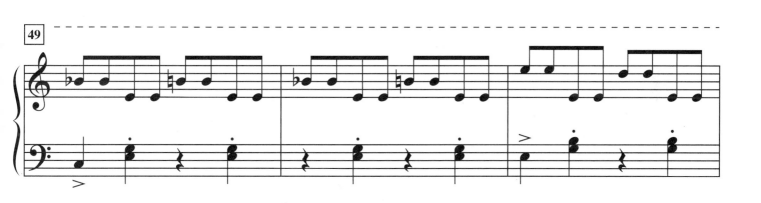

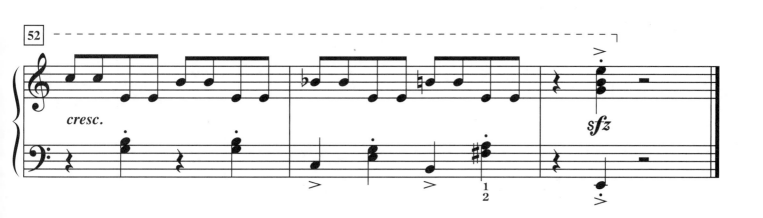

Dumbledore's Army
from *Harry Potter and the Order of the Phoenix*

Music by Nicholas Hooper
Arr. by Dan Coates

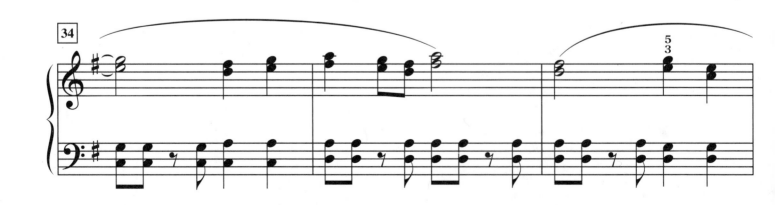

Loved Ones and Leaving
from *Harry Potter and the Order of the Phoenix*

Music by Nicholas Hooper

Arr. by Dan Coates

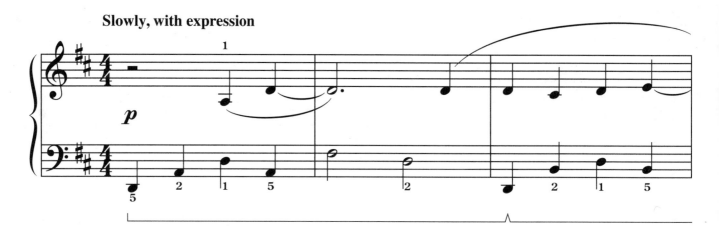

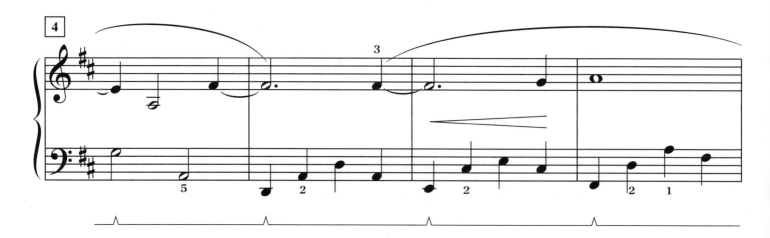

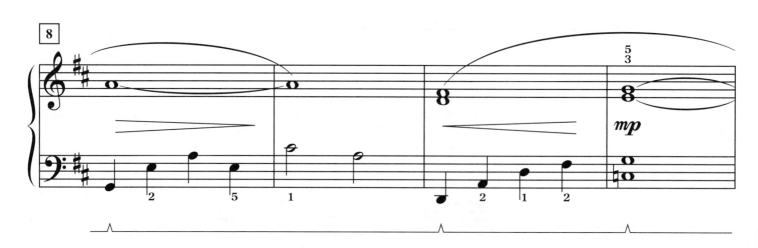

In Noctem

from *Harry Potter and the Half-Blood Prince*

Music by Nicholas Hooper
Lyrics by Steve Kloves

Arr. by Dan Coates

Harry and Hermione

from *Harry Potter and the Half-Blood Prince*

Music by Nicholas Hooper

Arr. by Dan Coates

Moderately slow

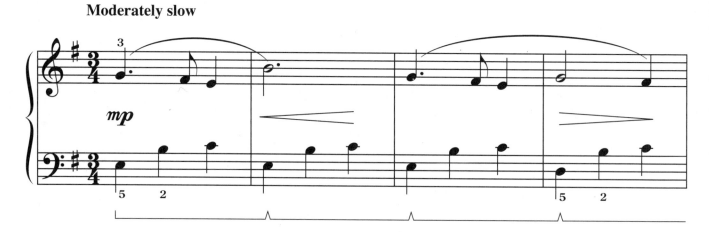

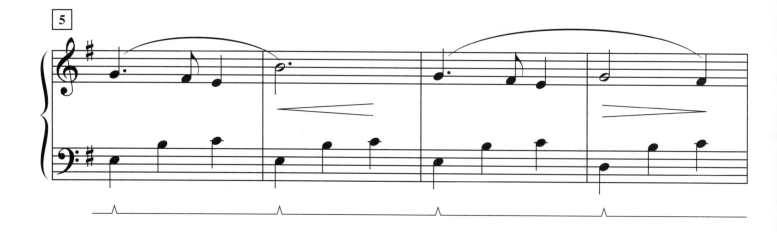

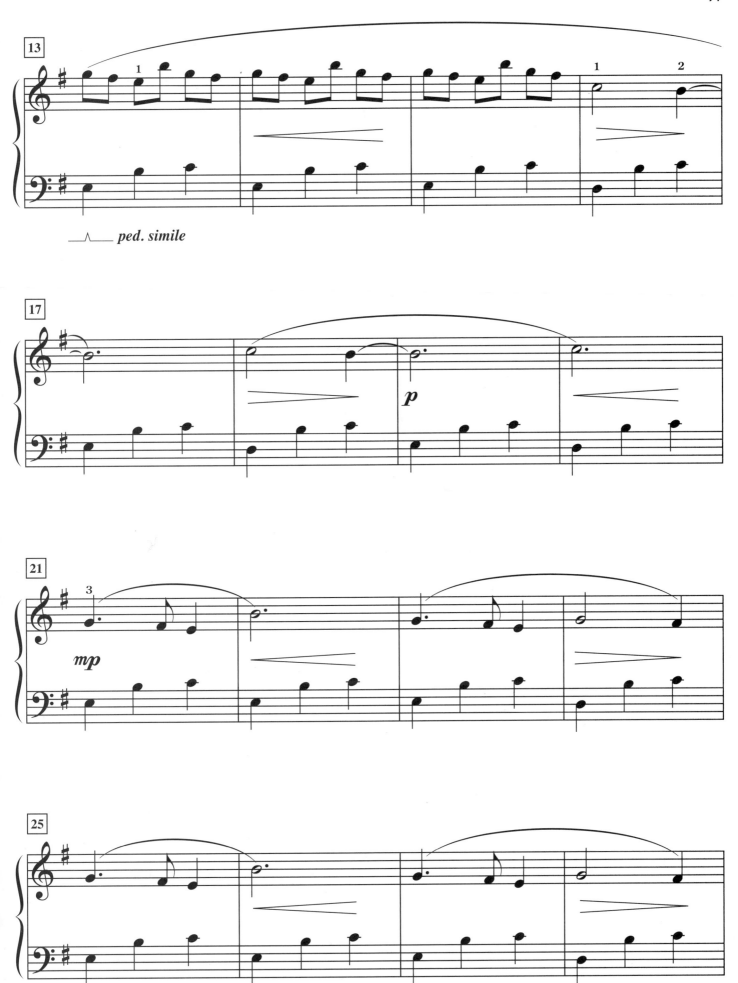

ped. simile

When Ginny Kissed Harry
from *Harry Potter and the Half-Blood Prince*

Music by Nicholas Hooper

Arr. by Dan Coates

Dumbledore's Farewell

from *Harry Potter and the Half-Blood Prince*

Music by Nicholas Hooper

Arr. by Dan Coates

Slowly, with expression

Obliviate
from *Harry Potter and the Deathly Hallows, Part 1*

By Alexandre Desplat

Arr. by Dan Coates

Moderately slow

Snape to Malfoy Manor

from *Harry Potter and the Deathly Hallows, Part 1*

By Alexandre Desplat

Arr. by Dan Coates

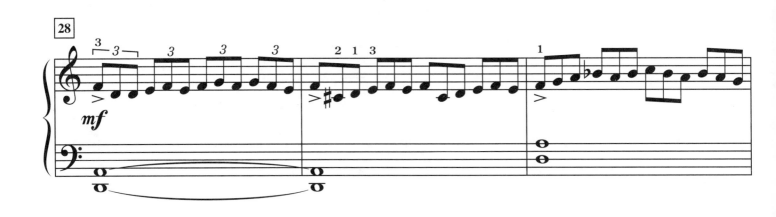

Ron Leaves

from *Harry Potter and the Deathly Hallows, Part 1*

By Alexandre Desplat

Arr. by Dan Coates

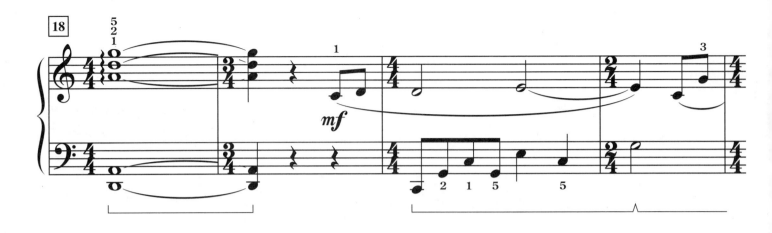

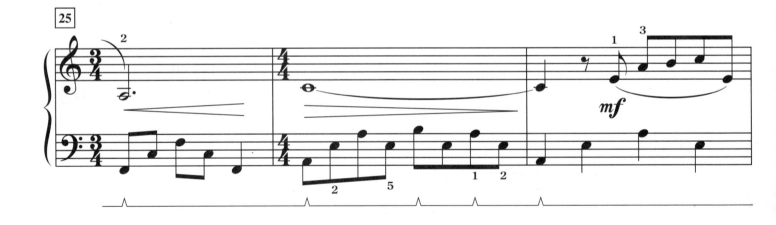

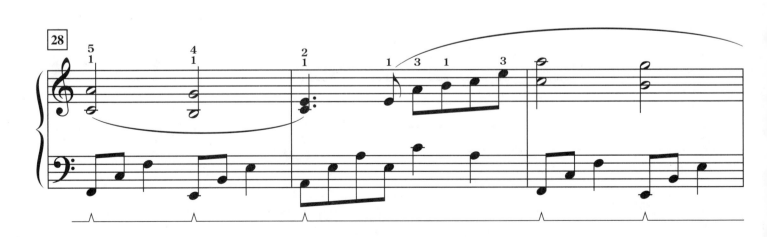

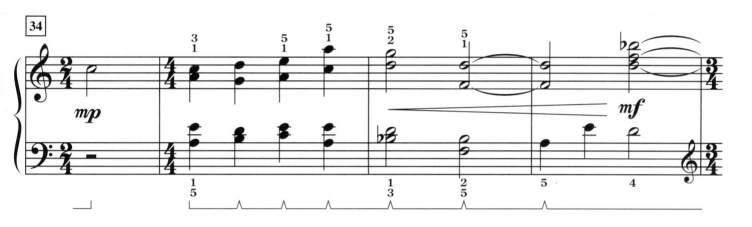

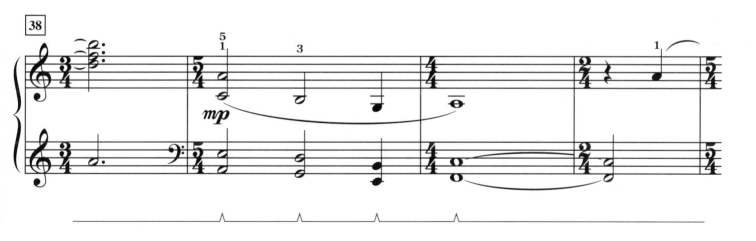

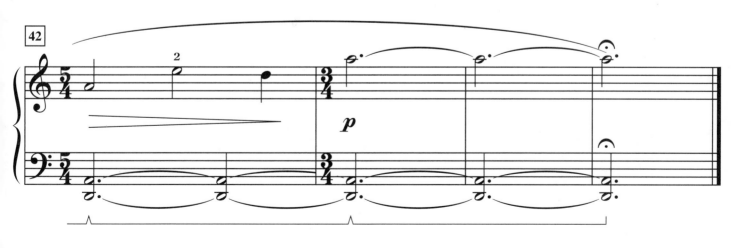

Harry and Ginny

from *Harry Potter and the Deathly Hallows, Part 1*

By Alexandre Desplat

Arr. by Dan Coates

Slowly and tenderly

Godric's Hollow Graveyard

from *Harry Potter and the Deathly Hallows, Part 1*

By Alexandre Desplat

Arr. by Dan Coates

Farewell to Dobby

from *Harry Potter and the Deathly Hallows, Part 1*

By Alexandre Desplat

Arr. by Dan Coates

Moderately slow

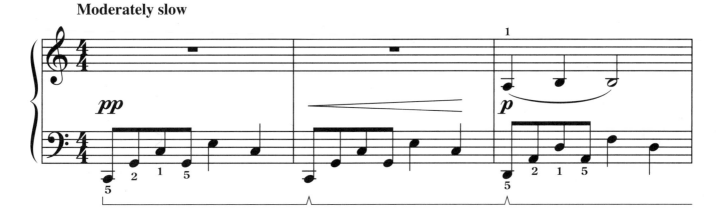

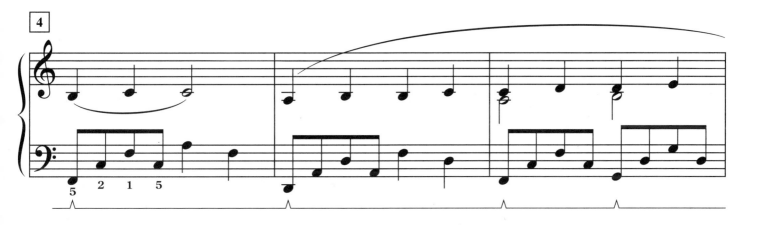

Lily's Theme
Main Theme from *Harry Potter and the Deathly Hallows, Part 2*

By Alexandre Desplat

Arr. by Dan Coates

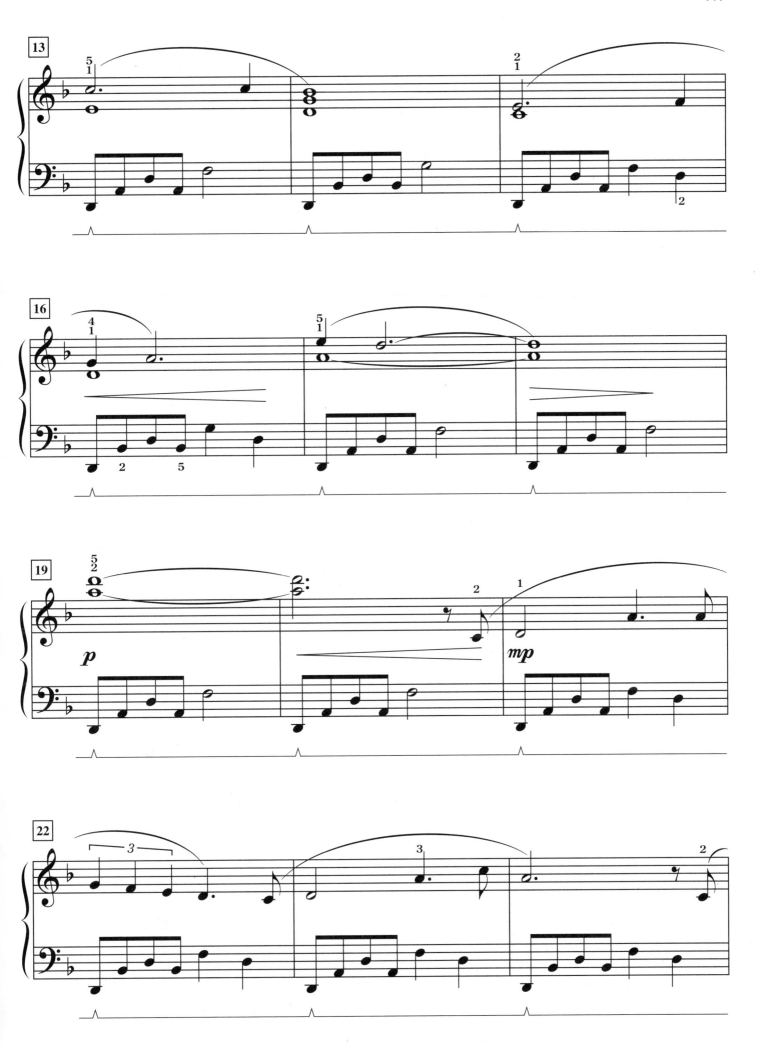

Courtyard Apocalypse
from *Harry Potter and the Deathly Hallows, Part 2*

By Alexandre Desplat

Arr. by Dan Coates

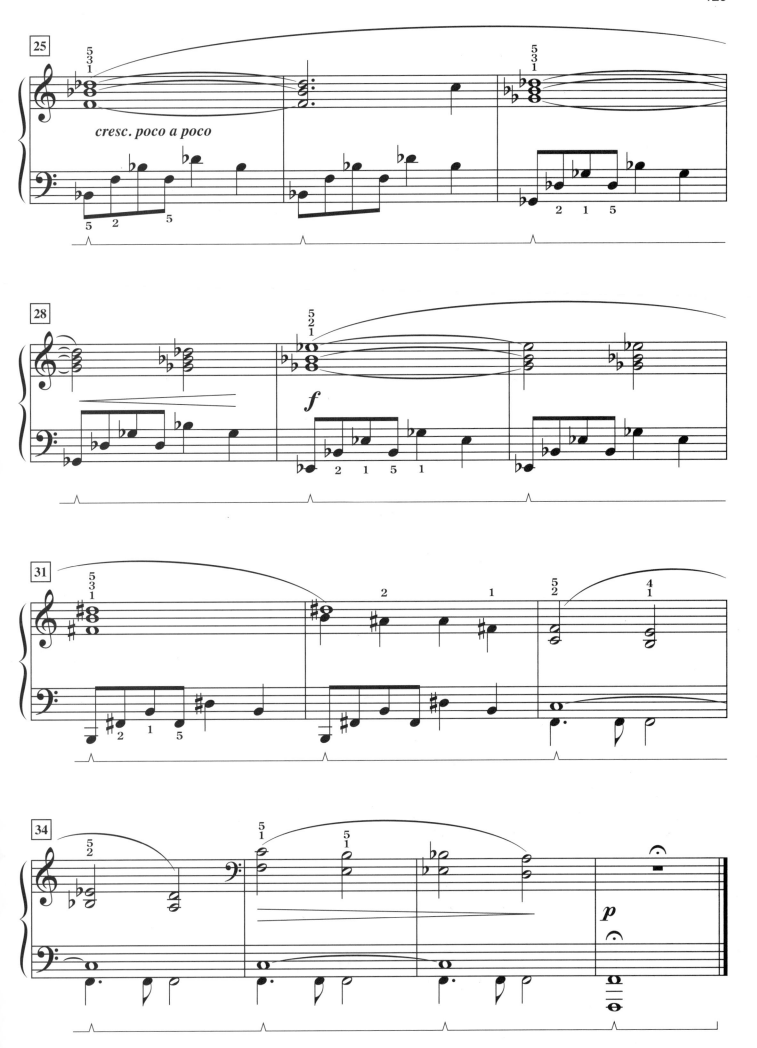

Statues

from *Harry Potter and the Deathly Hallows, Part 2*

By Alexandre Desplat

Arr. by Dan Coates

Moderately, with movement

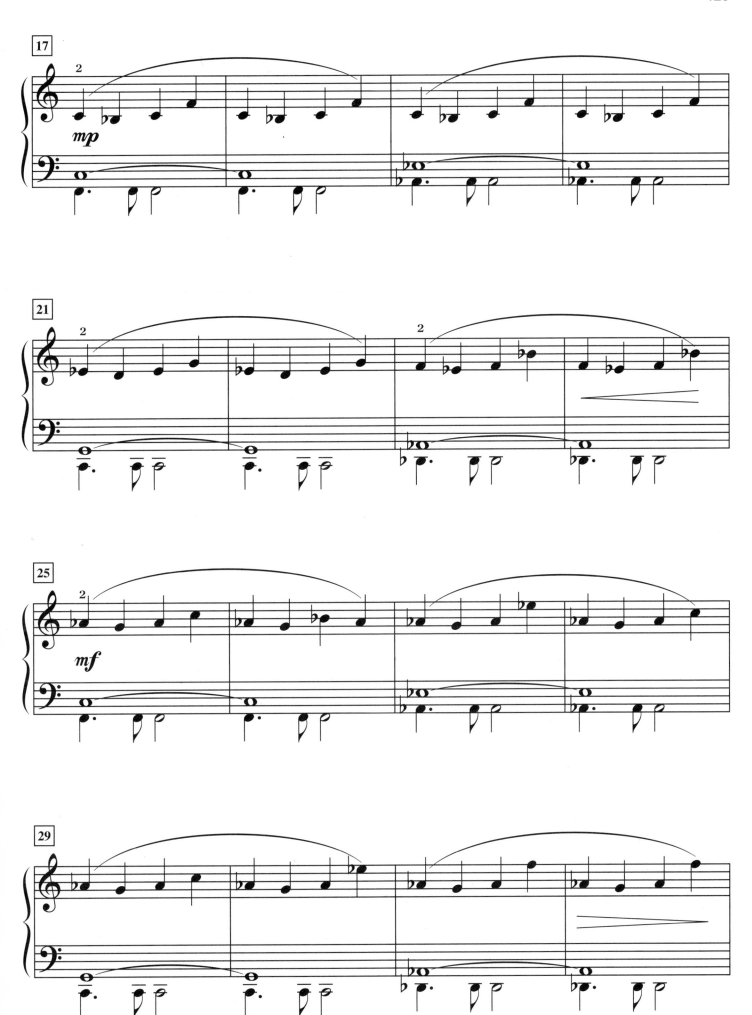

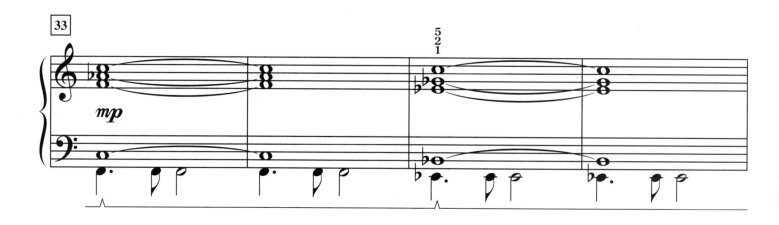

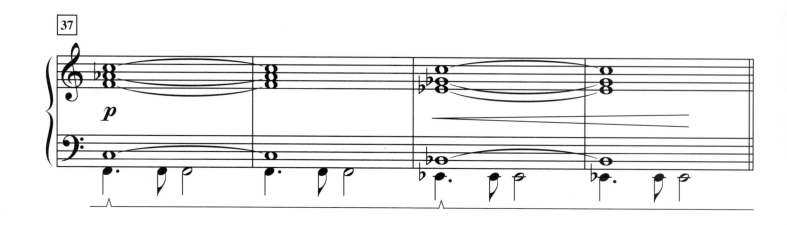

Severus and Lily

from *Harry Potter and the Deathly Hallows, Part 2*

By Alexandre Desplat

Arr. by Dan Coates

Harry's Sacrifice

from *Harry Potter and the Deathly Hallows, Part 2*

By Alexandre Desplat

Arr. by Dan Coates

A New Beginning

from *Harry Potter and the Deathly Hallows, Part 2*

By Alexandre Desplat

Arr. by Dan Coates

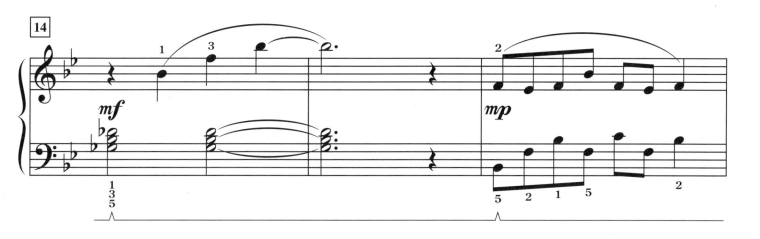

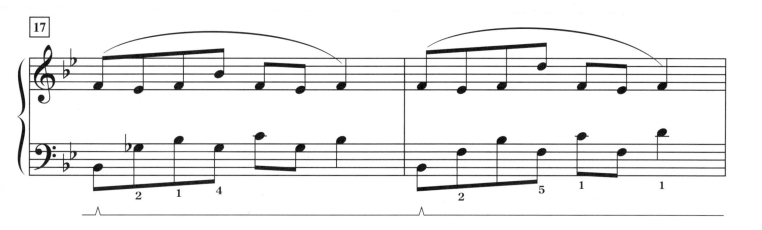

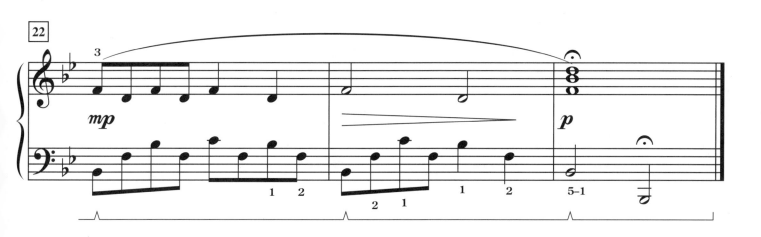

Lily's Lullaby
from *Harry Potter and the Deathly Hallows, Part 2*

By Alexandre Desplat

Arr. by Dan Coates

Moderately slow

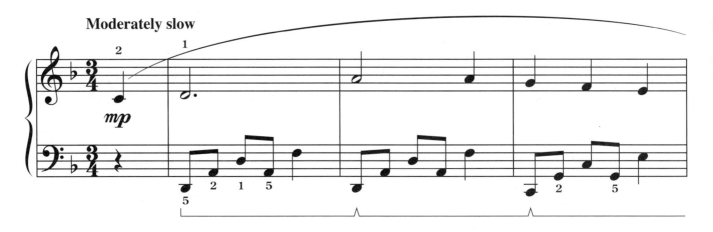

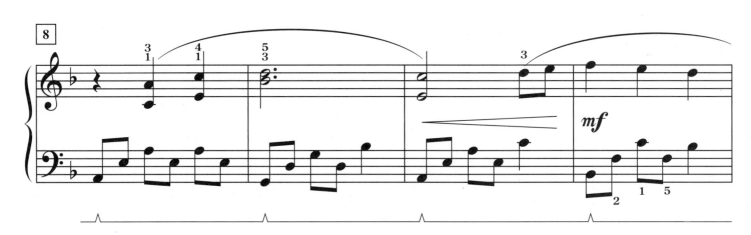